simply
Asian

Editor: Kelsey Lane
Layout and typesetting: Patty Holden
Cover: Patty Holden
Copy editing: Elizabeth Penn
Index preparation: Jonathan Silverman

Printed in Hong Kong

ISBN 1-930603-71-1

Nutritional analysis computations
are approximate.

Table of Contents

It's impossible to capture the entire, rich culinary heritage of the Asian continent in one basic cookbook. That said, even the tip of the iceberg of Asian cooking makes for an enticing, delicious journey. *Simply Asian* is designed to represent the heart and soul of many diverse cultures such as China, Japan, India, and the Southeast Asian countries of Vietnam, Thailand, Malaysia, and Indonesia.

You'll find a breadth of offerings from these locales, from familiar recipes such as Satay Skewers with Peanut Sauce (p. 18) and Sweet and Sour Pork (p. 112) to more exotic, adventurous ones like Clams in Sake Sauce (p. 86) and Malaysian Vegetable Soup (p. 62). Some recipes are central to one country, such as Indonesian Gado Gado (p. 68), while others blend the spirit of many Asian cultures into one dish—as in Asian-Pesto Fish Fillets (p. 72).

Asia is recognized worldwide for its clean, fresh, and visually appetizing cuisines—and for a focus on produce, rice, noodles, and seafood. Some characteristic Asian aromatics and herbs are ginger, chiles, lemon grass, cilantro, mint, and galangal. Add earthy, brewed soy sauce and fermented fish sauce and you create a flavor layer with intriguing depth.

One country like Vietnam may focus on light and fresh foods, while another such as India centers around gastronomic contrasts—smoothness with pungency, spiciness with refreshment, and so on.

Though every Asian country is unique, it's hard to overlook the similarities. It's those shared ingredients, tastes, and techniques we've brought together here.

Starters

Many Asian cultures, such as Japan, typically do not conduct meals in courses like we do—rather, they place all dishes on the table at once—unless they are partaking of an extremely formal dinner. However, myriad Asian dishes qualify beautifully as a small bite to get the appetite going.

Southeast Asian countries in particular are known for street food—delectable, Asian snacks, eaten on the run. These tasty morsels most easily translate into our American concept of a first course. Just visualize yourself in the middle of a Singaporean open-air market, with vivid colors, aromas, and bustling noises—and you're on your way.

For using this book to its full potential, here are some handy items to have on hand—some familiar, and some obscure:

Bamboo steamer

Wok

Chinese "spider," skimmer, or other slotted metal utensil for retrieving deep fried foods

Metal tongs

Table-top gas burner

Oil thermometer, for deep frying

Pastry blender, for cutting butter into flour

Chinese Chile-Garlic Sauce (Chinese grocery)

Sambal Oelek (Asian grocery)

Kecap Manis (sweet soy sauce, Asian grocery)

Nam Pla (fish sauce, also called nuoc nam; Asian grocery)

Fried Shrimp with Tamarind Sauce

Serves 6:
1 tablespoon tamarind paste
2 red onions
5 cloves garlic
1 fresh red chile pepper or ½ teaspoon crushed red pepper flakes
1 pound uncooked, peeled and de-veined shrimp
4¼ cups vegetable oil for deep-frying
1 tablespoon brown sugar
2 teaspoons fish sauce
1 teaspoon rice vinegar
1 egg white
Salt (preferably kosher or sea)
2 tablespoons cornstarch

Prep time: 50 minutes
Per serving approx: 294 calories
17 g fat/20 g fat/12 g carbohydrates

Stir tamarind paste into ½ cup hot tap water; set aside. Peel onions and garlic; finely chop both. Rinse chile pepper, remove stem, and mince (always wear gloves when dealing with hot peppers). Remove tails from shrimp; rinse and pat dry (if using frozen shrimp, thaw first according to package directions).

Heat oil in a pot to 350–375°F, testing with an oil thermometer (you can also test by inserting the end of a wooden spoon—bubbles should rise to the surface). Combine onions, garlic, chile, tamarind mixture, and brown sugar in a pot; bring to a boil, then reduce heat and simmer for about 5 minutes. Add fish sauce and vinegar, stir, and remove from heat. Sauce is finished.

Combine egg white and salt and dip each shrimp in the egg-white mixture. Then dust lightly with cornstarch using a small, fine-mesh strainer. Deep-fry shrimp in hot oil for about 2 minutes or until golden. Remove with a metal, slotted spoon (or other metal utensil), drain briefly, and serve immediately with the tamarind sauce.

Gyoza
Japanese Pot Stickers

Serves 8:

Gyoza:

40 round won ton wrappers (refrigerator section of supermarket)

1 piece ginger (¾ inch)

1 leek

8–12 spears fresh chives

¾ pound lean ground pork

1 tablespoon rice wine

2 tablespoons soy sauce

2 teaspoons rice vinegar

1 teaspoon sesame oil

Salt (preferably kosher or sea)

Sauce:

⅓ cup rice vinegar

⅓ cup soy sauce

2 teaspoons sesame oil (or more to taste)

Prep time: 1¼ hours

Per serving approx: 187 calories

10 g protein/4 g fat/27 g carbohydrates

PREPARE THE FILLING: Peel ginger and grate. Trim root end and any dark-green wilted parts from leek; slit open lengthwise, rinse well, and chop finely. Rinse chives, shake dry, and mince.

In a bowl, combine ground pork, ginger, leek, chives, rice wine, soy sauce, rice vinegar, sesame oil, and salt; mix until well-combined.

Distribute filling on top of wonton wrappers. Fold dough over the top into the shape of crescents (half moons), lightly wet the edges, and seal firmly together.

Bring a large pot of salted water to a boil. Throw in gyoza; return to a boil, then reduce heat to medium and cook for about 4 minutes. Remove with a slotted spoon.

SAUCE: mix rice vinegar, soy sauce, and sesame oil. Transfer to small bowls (one for each person). Or place a bowl of the dipping sauce on one large platter, surrounded by gyoza.

Serves 6–8:

Rice balls:

⅔ cup medium-grain rice, rinsed then soaked overnight

2 cloves garlic, minced

1 piece ginger (¾ inch), peeled and grated

2 sprigs fresh cilantro, minced (1 tablespoon)

1 pound lean ground pork

1 egg white

3 tablespoons soy sauce

1 tablespoon rice wine (mirin)

1 teaspoon sugar

Dumplings:

2 cups flour, plus more as needed

½ tablespoon butter

Pinch of salt (preferably kosher or sea)

6 dried shiitake mushrooms

1 small head napa cabbage (Chinese cabbage), chopped

2 tablespoons vegetable oil

2 tablespoons rice wine

2 tablespoons soy sauce

2 teaspoons sesame oil

½ teaspoon hot chili oil

Prep time: 1¾ hours (plus overnight soaking)

Per serving (8 servings) approx (rice balls): 201 calories

13 g protein/10 g fat/15 g carbohydrates

Per serving (8 servings) approx (dumplings): 179 calories

4 g protein/6 g fat/27 g carbohydrates

DUMPLINGS: Using a pastry blender, cut butter into flour. Mix in salt and 6 tablespoons warm water. Knead into a ball, cover with a cloth, and let stand for 30 plus minutes. Meanwhile, soak shiitake mushrooms in hot water.

RICE BALLS: Mix garlic, ginger, cilantro, pork, egg white, soy sauce, rice wine, and sugar; shape into walnut-sized balls. Drain rice and distribute on a plate. Roll balls in rice until coated. Place in a bamboo steamer and cover.

DUMPLINGS: Rinse shiitake mushrooms and pat dry; slice thinly. Sauté cabbage and shiitake in oil for about 5 minutes. Add rice wine, soy sauce, sesame oil, and chili oil; remove from heat. Knead dough and form into walnut-sized balls; roll each out thinly on lightly floured surface. Place some cabbage filling in the middle and cinch dough at the top, twisting slightly. Cover dumplings with a non-terry dish towel.

BOTH: Bring 1 inch of water to a boil in large pot or wok (the bamboo steamer bottom must fit inside). Position steamer (with rice balls) in the pot, cover, and steam over medium heat for 30 minutes. Add hot water for steaming as necessary.

Remove rice balls, and place dumplings in the steamer. Steam for 10 minutes. Serve with soy sauce, gyoza sauce (p. 10), or purchased Chinese chile-garlic sauce.

Serves 6:

Wraps:

3½ ounces cellophane noodles
1 pound cooked chicken
½ pound surimi (also called kamaboko, imitation crab)
1 cucumber
2 carrots
1 ripe avocado
6 green onions
¾ cup fresh mint sprigs
¾ cup fresh basil sprigs
⅔ cup roasted salted peanuts
½ cup bean sprouts, rinsed
1 head iceberg or 2 heads butter (or bibb) lettuce

Sauce:

¼ cup sugar
½ cup soy sauce
½ cup rice vinegar

Optional accompaniments:

Chinese chile-garlic sauce, soy sauce, sesame oil, Japanese pickled ginger

Prep time: 45 minutes
Per serving approx: 439 calories
20 g protein/23 g fat/45 g carbohydrates

Soak cellophane noodles in hot water for 10 minutes. Tear cooked chicken into strips. Slice surimi thinly.

Rinse and peel cucumber, trim ends, and halve lengthwise. Scrape out seeds with a spoon and slice rest crosswise thinly. Peel carrots; first cut lengthwise into thin slices and then into 1-inch sections. Halve avocado, remove pit, and cut flesh into thin wedges. Remove roots and any wilted parts from green onions, rinse, and cut into 1-inch sections and then into fine lengthwise strips.

Rinse herbs, shake dry, and discard any tough stems. Chop nuts. Discard lettuce core and rinse leaves; pat dry.

SAUCE: Mix sugar, soy sauce, and vinegar; heat only to melt sugar. Place all ingredients on the table.

For the meal, each person lays one lettuce leaf on a plate, fills it with ingredients as desired; rolls it up, and dips it in the sauce (or uses optional condiments).

Fresh Spring Rolls with Tofu

Serves 4:
Spring Rolls:
16 dried rice paper wrappers (8½-inch diameter)
8 lettuce leaves
8 ounces firm tofu
1 tablespoon fish sauce
Chili powder:
½ cup vegetable oil for pan-frying
4 white cabbage leaves
½ cup bean sprouts
½ cup fresh mint sprigs
½ cup fresh cilantro sprigs
Sauce:
1 fresh red chile (Fresno, serrano, or jalapeño)
2 cloves garlic
1 piece ginger (¾ inch)
2 tablespoons roasted salted peanuts
1 teaspoon sugar
1 tablespoon fish sauce
1 tablespoon rice vinegar
2 tablespoons soy sauce

Prep time: 50 minutes
Per serving approx: 290 calories
6 g protein/14 g fat/38 g carbohydrates

Fill a large bowl with lukewarm water. Dip rice paper wrappers one at a time until pliable. Remove, lay side by side on a clean work surface, and cover with a damp dishtowel.

Rinse lettuce leaves, pat dry, and pare down any thick ribs (flatten leaves). Cut tofu into strips ½-inch thick; brush with fish sauce and dust with chili powder. Pat dry. Heat oil in a pan and fry tofu strips until golden. Drain on paper towels.

Rinse cabbage leaves, sprouts, and herbs; drain. Cut cabbage into strips. Trim tough stems from herbs.

Stack rice paper wrappers two high, top with 1 lettuce leaf and some each of the cabbage, sprouts, herbs, and fried tofu. Fold wrapper edges over the filling and roll up the rice paper wrappers tightly. Arrange on a platter.

For the dipping sauce, rinse chile pepper and remove stem (always wear gloves when working with hot peppers, and don't touch your face); mince rest. Omit seeds and ribs for less heat. Peel garlic and ginger; finely chop both along with peanuts. Mix sugar, fish sauce, rice vinegar, and soy sauce; stir in chopped ingredients. Serve with spring rolls.

Satay Skewers

Serves 6–8:

1½ pounds meat or poultry (e.g., pork, leg of lamb, chicken breast)
1 piece ginger (¾ inch)
¼ cup soy sauce
¼ cup kecap manis (sweet, seasoned soy sauce found in Asian markets)
3 tablespoons oil (if sautéing)

Peanut sauce:
¾ cup roasted salted peanuts
2 tablespoons oil
2 tablespoons red curry paste
1 cup coconut milk
2 tablespoons brown sugar
Salt (preferably kosher or sea)
2 tablespoons lime juice

Prep time: 50 minutes (plus 2 hours marinating)
Per serving (8) approx: 314 calories
15 g protein/26 g fat/9 g carbohydrates

Slice meat very thinly and thread it back and forth onto long wooden or metal skewers like an accordion (pre-soak wooden skewers in water for one hour prior). Peel ginger, grate finely, and mix with soy sauce and kecap manis; distribute over skewers. Cover and marinate for at least 2 hours.

SAUCE: Chop or grind peanuts very finely. Heat oil in a pot and add curry paste; sauté briefly. Add coconut milk, ½ cup water, peanuts, and sugar, and simmer over medium heat for 10–15 minutes. Season sauce to taste with salt and lime juice; let cool to lukewarm.

Cook the skewers either on a charcoal grill, under an oven broiler, or in a pan with oil over high heat. In any case, cook only until the meat is lightly browned (make sure pork and chicken are cooked fully throughout). Serve peanut sauce alongside.

Indian Pakoras

Serves 4:
2⅔ cups chickpea flour
Salt (preferably kosher or sea)
1 teaspoon vegetable oil plus 4¼ cups for deep-frying
2 jalapeños
½ cup fresh mint sprigs
1 cup (8 ounces) yogurt
½ teaspoon ground cumin
1¾ pounds vegetables (e.g., potatoes, cauliflower, broccoli, eggplant, zucchini)
A few uncooked shrimp (optional), peeled and deveined

Prep time: 35 minutes
Per serving approx: 624 calories
22 g protein/35 g fat/59 g carbohydrates

For the batter, combine chickpea flour with a few pinches salt. Add 1 teaspoon vegetable oil to 1 cup lukewarm water and whisk mixture into chickpea flour until it forms a thick batter. Set aside.

YOGURT DIP: Rinse jalapeños, discard stem, and chop rest (omit seeds and ribs for less heat; always wear gloves when working with hot peppers). Rinse mint, shake dry, and chop. Purée yogurt, mint, and chiles in a blender. Season dip to taste with salt and cumin.

Peel or rinse vegetables and cut into bite-size chunks (slice potatoes to ¼-inch thick). Rinse shrimp and pat dry.

Set oven to 170°F and warm a large platter inside. Heat the 4¼ cups oil, in a high-sided pot, to 350–375°F (use an oil thermometer). Or, to test readiness of oil, lower the handle of a wooden spoon down into the oil. If bubbles congregate around the handle, it's hot enough.

Gradually dip vegetables (and shrimp) in the batter to coat (if too thick, whisk in more lukewarm water). Deep-fry pieces in hot oil for about 4 minutes, until golden. Remove with a slotted metal utensil, drain on oven-warmed platter (lined with paper towels), and then keep warm in the oven until remaining vegetables are fried. Serve yogurt dip alongside.

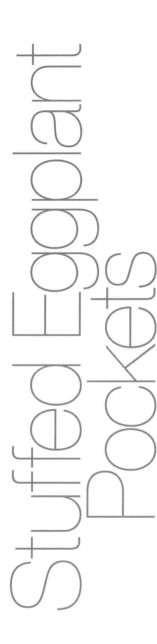

Stuffed Eggplant Pockets

Serves 4:

Pockets:

1 piece ginger (¾ inch)
4 green onions
5 ounces ground pork
1 tablespoon rice wine
Salt (preferably kosher or sea)
2 eggplants (about 8 ounces each)
2 eggs
1½ tablespoons cornstarch
3½ cups oil for deep-frying

Sauce:

½ teaspoon crushed red pepper flakes (or to taste)
2 tablespoons rice vinegar
2 teaspoons sesame oil
¼ cup soy sauce
2 teaspoons sugar

Prep time: 40 minutes
Per serving approx: 395 calories
13 g protein/29 g fat/23 g carbohydrates

Peel ginger and grate. Remove root ends and any wilted parts from green onions, rinse, and chop very finely. Mix together grated ginger, green onions, ground pork, and rice wine; season with salt.

Peel eggplants with a vegetable peeler and cut into ½-inch-thick rounds. Slice each round open crosswise to form a fillable pocket—without cutting all the way through so the halves hold together. Fill each pocket with some pork mixture and press closed.

Whisk together eggs, cornstarch, and salt thoroughly. Heat oil in a wide pot to 350–375°F (use oil thermometer).

FOR THE SAUCE: Combine crushed red pepper flakes, rice vinegar, sesame oil, soy sauce, and sugar. Mix well.

Set oven to 170°F and warm an oven-safe platter inside. Dip eggplant pockets into the egg mixture and then deep-fry for about 4 minutes, until golden, turning occasionally with metal tongs. Remove with a slotted metal spoon or skimmer and transfer to the oven-warmed platter (lined with paper towels). Warm in oven until remaining eggplant pockets are fried.

Serve sauce alongside, or drizzle sauce on top.

Crispy Vegetable Parcels with Tomato Dip

Serves 4:

Dough:
1¾ cup flour, plus more
for work surface
Salt (preferably kosher or sea)
1 egg
3 tablespoons vegetable oil
plus more for frying

Dip:
2 large ripe tomatoes
1–2 red chile peppers
(e.g., Fresno, serrano, jalapeño)
4 cloves garlic
3 tablespoons grated coconut
1 tablespoon lime juice
Salt (preferably kosher or sea)

Filling:
5 green onions, rinsed
½ pound green beans
Salt (preferably kosher or sea)
¼ pound shiitake mushrooms
5 leaves napa (Chinese)
cabbage
1 piece ginger (¾ inch)
2 tablespoons vegetable oil
½ pound ground beef
1 teaspoon sambal oelek
(Asian market)
1 tablespoon soy sauce
1 egg

Prep time: 1½ hours
Per serving approx: 544 calories
17 g protein/29 g fat/
56 g carbohydrates

DOUGH: Combine flour and salt; add egg, oil, and about 3½ tablespoons water and mix together. Knead dough thoroughly on lightly floured surface until soft, pliable, and smooth. If sticky, add flour; if dry, add water. Shape into a ball, cover with a damp dishtowel, and let rest 1 hour.

DIP: Cover tomatoes (cored) with boiling water. Let stand briefly, then rinse, slip off skins, and chop rest. Rinse chiles, discard stems, and chop rest finely. Peel garlic and squeeze through a press. Mix all dip ingredients together.

FILLING: Slice white part of green onions into fine rings. Rinse beans, trim ends, and cut in thirds; simmer in salted water for 5 minutes. Drain and rinse with cold water.

Wipe mushrooms with paper towels. Discard mushroom stems and slice caps. Rinse Chinese cabbage and chop. Peel ginger and grate.

Heat oil and sauté green onions and ginger briefly. Add mushrooms; stir. Then add beef; stir-fry until crumbly. Add Chinese cabbage and beans, cooking until cabbage softens. Season with sambal oelek, soy sauce, and salt; let cool. Stir in egg.

ASSEMBLY: Divide dough into eight equal pieces; roll out thinly on a lightly floured surface into rectangles. Top half of each rectangle with filling, fold over the other half, and press edges together; notch with a fork.

Heat ½ inch of oil in bottom of a wide pan (350–375°F); pan-fry four parcels over medium heat for 4 minutes, turning once, until golden. Warm first batch on an oven-safe platter in a 170°F oven while finishing second batch. Serve dip alongside.

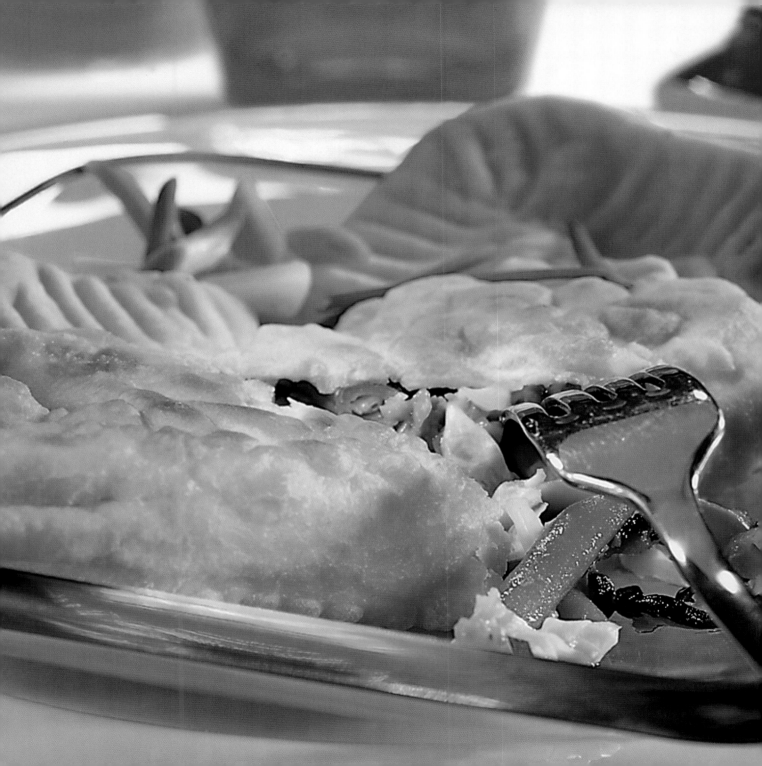

Serves 8:
6 tablespoons sesame seeds
10–12 ounces non-raw fish (e.g., water-packed tuna, smoked salmon, cooked shrimp)
2 tablespoons Japanese pickled ginger
5 sheets seasoned, roasted seaweed (nori)
¼ cup red caviar (tobiko)
1 batch sushi rice (see below)
⅓ cup rice vinegar for shaping
Japanese soy sauce and wasabi (from a tube) for dipping

Prep time: 30 minutes
Per serving approx: 486 calories
65 g protein/7 g fat/38 g carbohydrates

Toast sesame seeds in a dry pan and set aside. Break fish into small pieces. Chop pickled ginger. Coarsely crumble 1 sheet seaweed. Cut remaining sheets into strips ½-inch wide using kitchen shears.

Loosely mix together fish, crumbled nori, pickled ginger, 2 tablespoons of the toasted sesame seeds, 2 tablespoons of the red caviar, and sushi rice. Combine ⅓ cup water and the rice vinegar; use for moistening your hands.

Form walnut-sized balls of the rice mixture with your hands. Roll balls in remaining sesame seeds and wrap each once around with a seaweed strip, shiny side out. Garnish with caviar. Stir together soy sauce and wasabi, and dip the onigiri into this sauce.

Sushi Rice

Soak and drain 1¾ cup sushi rice (short- or medium-grain) repeatedly in cold water until water runs clear. Drain in a colander for 1 hour. Bring rice and 2 cups plus 2 tablespoons water to a boil over high heat. Reduce heat to very low and add ⅓ cup cold water. After 5 more minutes, remove from heat; let sit for 10 minutes. Transfer to a bowl, fluff with a wooden spoon, and let cool. Bring ¼ cup rice vinegar to a boil with salt and 3 teaspoons sugar. Gradually add to lukewarm rice. Salt to taste. Prep time: 1¾ hours.

Hand-Rolled Sushi

Makes 16:
3 eggs
3 teaspoons sugar
2 tablespoons Japanese soy sauce, plus more for dipping
1 teaspoon vegetable oil
4 green onions
1 ripe avocado
½ cucumber
½ teaspoon fresh lemon juice
5 ounces tofu
½ cup bean sprouts
8 large sheets seasoned, roasted seaweed
1 batch sushi rice (see p. 26)
Wasabi (from a tube)
Mayonnaise for spreading

Prep time: 30 minutes (plus hand-rolling at the table)
Per serving approx: 270 calories
8 g protein/9 g fat/41 g carbohydrates

Mix eggs, sugar, and 1 tablespoon of the soy sauce. Brush a nonstick pan with oil; pour in egg mixture. Cover and cook on lowest possible heat for 5 minutes until set. Flip over in pan, turn off heat, and let cool.

Rinse green onions, trim wilted parts, and cut lengthwise into quarters; soak in ice water until serving time. Halve avocado, remove pit, scoop out flesh, and slice into ½-inch x 2-inch strips; brush with lemon juice. Peel cucumber, halve lengthwise, and remove seeds. Slice tofu and omelet into ½-inch x 2-inch strips; mix with remaining soy sauce.

Halve seaweed sheets. Place all ingredients on table, plus the sushi rice. Supply each guest with small saucers of water.

Each guest should: Lay out seaweed sheet, shiny side down. Using a wet spoon, spread the left half with a thin layer of rice. Spread on wasabi or mayonnaise and top with a few strips of desired ingredients. Then roll the seaweed around the filling tightly into a little cone; use a dab of water to press together. Drizzle with soy sauce, or dip, and enjoy.

Soups, Salads, and Vegetarian Dishes

As they are in America, dishes such as soups, salads, and vegetarian offerings are considered lighter fare in Asia. A soup may be used as a palate cleanser—a salad to provide a cooling sensation after the intensity of a spicy dish. And, vegetables across the board are indispensable in Asian cooking, as they are refreshing in nature. Some of the dishes we've included here are suitable as first courses or side dishes—like Cucumber-Fruit Salad (p. 46).

However, many of the recipes in this section can also be viewed as one-dish meals—even downright comfort food. Think miso soup (p. 34) on a cool November evening, or the silkiness of coconut sauce in Tofu-Vegetable Stir Fry over rice (p. 60).

Asian Soup Bases

Chinese Chicken Broth

Makes 2 quarts stock:
1 whole chicken (about 3 pounds)
5 ounces bacon or ham hock
1 leek, rinsed well and chopped coarsely
1 piece ginger (1½ inch), peeled and sliced
Zest of one orange
4–5 dried shiitake mushrooms, rinsed
1 star anise
1 teaspoon Sichuan peppercorns
2 tablespoons rice wine
Salt (preferably kosher or sea)

Prep time: 1¾ hours

Rinse chicken inside and out, drain, and place in a large pot with bacon; cover with about 2 quarts cold water and heat.

Add the leek, ginger, orange zest, and shiitakes. Tie star anise and Sichuan peppercorns in a cheesecloth pouch—add to stock. Simmer over low heat (just below a boil) for 1¼ hours, partially covered. Add rice wine and salt to taste.

Let chicken cool in the stock (to lukewarm), then remove (use cooked chicken for other recipes). Pour stock through a fine mesh strainer and refrigerate. Remove any fat that forms on top. Freeze any stock you don't intend to use right away.

Japanese Dashi Stock

Makes 1 quart dashi:
1 sheet (⅓ ounce) kombu (dark, hard seaweed—also called kelp; Japanese market)
2 dried shiitake mushrooms, rinsed briefly
⅔ ounce bonito flakes (smoked, dried fish shavings; Japanese market)

Prep time: 15 minutes

Cut up kombu and mushrooms with kitchen shears. This will help to release flavor during the short cooking time.

Place both ingredients in a pot with no more than 1 quart water and bring to a boil slowly over medium-high heat.

When boiling, remove kombu and shiitake; add a shot of cold water so the stock will stop bubbling. Next add the bonito flakes and return to a boil. Remove from heat, let stand briefly, and pour through a fine mesh strainer. Ready to use.

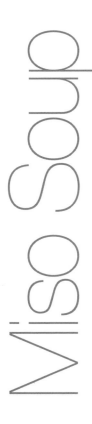

Miso Soup

Serves 4:
4 ounces tofu
2 tender leeks
3 cups dashi stock (recipe page 32)
3 ounces medium-dark miso

Prep time: 10 minutes
Per serving approx: 214 calories
10 g protein/6 g fat/33 g carbohydrates

Cut tofu into ¾-inch uniform cubes. Remove root end and darkest green parts from leeks, rinse, and slice on a slight diagonal into very thin rings. Rinse leek rings again, well, in a colander.

Heat dashi stock in a pot to just before boiling. Push miso through a strainer into the hot dashi; stir well. Do not allow to boil—very important.

Add tofu and leeks to pot; heat until both are warmed through. Serve miso soup.

Japanese Shabu Shabu

Serves 4:
1⅓ pounds ribeye steak
2 ounces cellophane noodles
8 ounces firm tofu
½ small head napa (Chinese) cabbage
1 cup spinach, rinsed
2 leeks
7 ounces shiitake or oyster mushrooms
2 carrots
½ daikon radish
About 1 quart dashi stock (page 32 or instant)

Ponzu sauce:
⅓ cup soy sauce
2 tablespoons lemon juice
3 tablespoons rice wine (sake, mirin)

Miso-sesame sauce:
3 tablespoons sesame seeds
1½ tablespoons light miso
1 tablespoon sugar
¼ cup rice vinegar
¼ cup rice wine (sake, mirin)
¼ cup soy sauce
Hot mustard to taste
¼ cup dashi stock (page 32 or instant), heated

Prep time: 45 minutes
(plus 1 hour freezing time)
Per serving approx:
918 calories
43 g protein/38 g fat/
103 g carbohydrates

Freeze beef, wrapped, for 1 hour.

Cover cellophane noodles with hot water, soak for 5 minutes, and then drain in a colander; halve using kitchen shears. Cube tofu uniformly.

Core napa cabbage and discard any wilted parts; slice into fine strips. Rinse spinach well; trim tough stems. Remove root end and any wilted parts from leeks; rinse, cut into strips ½ inch x 2 inches. Discard mushroom stems; wipe caps with a paper towel and slice thinly. Peel carrots and slice very thinly on a slight diagonal. Peel daikon and grate finely.

Transfer grated daikon to a small bowl and arrange remaining ingredients decoratively on large platters.

Remove ribeye from freezer and slice thinly with sharp knife. Arrange slices on a platter. Heat dashi stock to a low boil.

Ponzu sauce: combine soy sauce, lemon juice, and rice wine. Miso sauce: toast sesame seeds in a dry pan briefly until a pale golden color. Grind briefly in a food processor, blender, or spice grinder. Mix with miso, sugar, rice vinegar, rice wine, soy sauce, mustard, and hot dashi stock. Transfer sauces to small bowls.

Transfer pot with hot dashi stock to an electric or gas burner at the table (or use fondue pot). Guests can cook ingredients in the hot stock using chopsticks and then dip cooked items into the sauces provided. The grated daikon is used as a condiment.

Thai Hot and Sour Shrimp Soup

Serves 4:
1 pound uncooked shell-on shrimp
2 stalks lemon grass
1 tablespoon dried shrimp (optional)
2 tablespoons vegetable oil
2/3 cup fresh cilantro sprigs
2 cloves garlic
1/8 teaspoon freshly ground black pepper
5 shiitake or oyster mushrooms
1 piece galangal (about 1/2 inch; or substitute ginger)
1/2 teaspoon crushed red pepper flakes
1/4 cup lime juice
4 kaffir lime leaves
1 tablespoon fish sauce
1 teaspoon sugar
2 green onions
Salt (preferably kosher or sea)

Prep time: 35 minutes
Per serving approx: 237 calories
26 g protein/10 g fat/10 g carbohydrates

Peel and de-vein shrimp, but rinse shells and reserve. Rinse shrimp and cut lengthwise into pieces 1/2-inch wide. Rinse 1 stalk of the lemon grass, remove outer layer, and cut rest into 1-inch sections

Sauté shrimp shells and dried shrimp in oil for a couple minutes until aromatic. Add lemon grass and 1 quart water; bring to a boil and cook for 15 minutes. Meanwhile, rinse cilantro, shake dry, and trim any tough stems. Peel garlic and coarsely chop. In a blender or small food processor, process garlic, cilantro, and black pepper (add a bit of water if necessary) to form a seasoning paste.

Discard mushroom stems; wipe off caps and thinly slice. Peel galangal and slice. Rinse remaining lemon grass, trim bottom and top ends, and remove outer later; cut the rest into rings.

Strain shrimp stock and return to the pot. Add crushed red pepper flakes, seasoning paste, lime juice, lemon grass rings, kaffir lime leaves, fish sauce, and sugar; return to a boil.

Stir in galangal, mushrooms, and raw shrimp; cook over medium heat for 2 minutes. Salt to taste. Trim roots and any wilted parts from green onions, rinse, and cut into very fine rings—use to garnish soup. Galangal, lemon grass, and kaffir lime leaves add flavor to each bowl of soup but are not meant to be eaten.

Rice Noodle Soup with Pork

Serves 4:
4 shallots
2 cloves garlic
2 jalapeños
1 teaspoon brown sugar
3½ ounces wide rice noodles
Salt (preferably kosher or sea)
¾ pound pork tenderloin or lean pork loin
3 tablespoons oil
1 tablespoon kecap manis (sweet soy sauce, Asian grocery store)
1 quart chicken stock (recipe page 32 or purchased variety)
2 tablespoons tamarind paste (from container/jar, Asian grocery store)
¾ cup bean sprouts
2 tablespoons fresh cilantro leaves
¼ cup roasted salted peanuts, chopped

Prep time: 25 minutes
Per serving approx: 492 calories
14 g protein/17 g fat/70 g carbohydrates

Peel shallots and garlic and chop both coarsely. Rinse jalapeños, discard stems and seeds, and chop rest coarsely. Purée shallots, garlic, jalapeños, and brown sugar using a hand blender, food processor, or blender (use a bit of water if necessary).

Cook noodles until al dente in lightly salted, boiling water (3–5 minutes). Drain and rinse with cold water.

Slice pork thinly. Heat 2 tablespoons of the oil in a wok or pan and brown meat briefly over high heat; remove from pan.

Heat remaining oil in pan; sauté the shallot purée. Season with kecap manis, pour in stock, and bring to a boil. Add tamarind paste; bring to a rolling boil.

Rinse and drain sprouts. Add to soup along with pork and rice noodles; simmer for a couple minutes until ingredients are warmed through. Salt to taste, and ladle into individual bowls. Garnish with cilantro and peanuts.

Thai Coconut Soup with Chicken

Serves 4:
¾ pound chicken breasts
1 tablespoon fish sauce
1 piece galangal (¾ inch; may substitute ginger)
2 stalks lemon grass
1 red Fresno chile pepper
4 firm medium tomatoes
1 can coconut milk (1⅔ cups)
2¼ cups chicken stock (recipe page 32 or purchased)
3 tablespoons lime or lemon juice
1 teaspoon sugar
3–4 sprigs cilantro

Prep time: 25 minutes
Per serving approx: 395 calories
16 g protein/31 g fat/18 g carbohydrates

Dice chicken finely, mix well with ½ tablespoon of the fish sauce, and set aside.

Peel galangal and slice thinly. Rinse lemon grass, remove outer layer, and cut rest into pieces 1-inch long. Rinse chile, discard stem, and cut rest into fine rings. Rinse and core tomatoes, and cut into eighths.

In a pot, combine coconut milk with stock and heat. Add galangal, lemon grass, chile, remaining fish sauce, citrus juice, and sugar. Simmer for 5 minutes.

Add diced chicken and tomatoes and simmer gently for another 5 plus minutes or until chicken is cooked through. Meanwhile, rinse cilantro, shake dry, and remove leaves from stems. Salt soup to taste, and garnish servings with cilantro leaves. Galangal and lemon grass add flavor to each bowl of soup but are not meant to be consumed (eating chile slices optional).

Glass Noodle Salad with Beef and Mushrooms

Serves 4:

6 dried porcini mushrooms, rinsed
3½ ounces cellophane (glass) noodles
2 fresh red chiles (Fresno, red serrano, or red jalapeño)
2 shallots
8 fresh chive spears
¼ pound oyster or white mushrooms
1 tablespoon fish sauce
1 tablespoon soy sauce
¼ cup lime or lemon juice
1 tablespoon sugar
2 tablespoons oil
½ pound ground beef

Prep time: 40 minutes
Per serving approx: 440 calories
7 g protein/14 g fat/74 g carbohydrates

Soak dried porcinis in warm water for 20 minutes. Soak cellophane noodles in hot water for only 10 minutes.

Rinse chiles, discard stems, and cut rest into fine rings. Peel shallots, cut in half, and then cut into strips. Rinse chives, pat dry, and cut into 1½-inch lengths. Wipe off mushrooms with paper towels, discard stems, and slice caps thinly.

Drain porcinis and rinse; remove stems and chop caps. Drain cellophane noodles and halve using kitchen shears.

Mix fish sauce, soy sauce, citrus juice, and sugar. Heat oil in a pan. Sauté porcinis and other mushrooms briefly over high heat. Add ground beef and fry until crumbly. Add chiles and shallots; sauté briefly. Stir in noodles and heat through for 1–2 minutes. Add fish sauce mixture and chives, stir well, and transfer to a bowl. Wait until lukewarm, then stir; salt to taste. Serve salad at room temperature or chilled.

Cucumber-Fruit Salad

Serves 4:
2 tablespoons dried shrimp (Asian grocery)
1 cucumber
1 small pineapple
1 mango
2 shallots
3 cloves garlic
3 red Fresno chile peppers (mildly hot)
1 tablespoon oil
1 tablespoon brown sugar
2 teaspoons fish sauce
1 teaspoon soy sauce
¼ cup lime juice
Salt (preferably kosher or sea)
Cilantro leaves for garnish

Prep time: 45 minutes
Per serving approx: 193 calories
7 g protein/5 g fat/35 g carbohydrates

Mix dried shrimp with 3½ tablespoons warm water; soak for about 30 minutes, then drain.

Rinse cucumber, trim ends, and cut lengthwise into quarters. Scrape out seeds with a spoon and slice quarters crosswise, ¼-inch thick. Peel pineapple and cut into slices, then into small chunks. Peel mango and cut fruit away from pit, then into small chunks. Mix cucumber, pineapple, and mango.

Peel shallots and garlic and chop both finely. Rinse chiles, discard stems, and cut rest into rings. Sauté shallots and garlic in oil for 2–3 minutes while stirring constantly. Add dried shrimp mixture, chiles, and brown sugar; continue sautéing until the brown sugar dissolves. Purée mixture along with fish sauce and soy sauce in a blender; let cool.

Add lime juice to puréed sauce, season with salt, and fold into cucumber and fruit mixture. Let salad marinate a little, then sprinkle with cilantro leaves, and serve.

Serves 4:

Dip:

2 tablespoons dried shrimp
2 cloves garlic, peeled
2 shallots, peeled
2 red Fresno chile peppers
¼ cup lime juice
1 tablespoon fish sauce
1 tablespoon soy sauce
1 tablespoon brown sugar

Vegetables:

1 section daikon radish (about ½ pound)
5 green onions
4 stalks celery
1 cucumber
2 carrots
6 spears green asparagus

Prep time: 40 minutes
Per serving approx: 112 calories
7 g protein/2 g fat/19 g carbohydrates

Rinse dried shrimp and soak in hot water for 30 minutes. Meanwhile, thoroughly rinse all vegetables, and peel carrots and daikon. Cut all vegetables into uniform sticks for dipping.

Drain shrimp and mince along with garlic and shallots. Rinse chiles, discard stems, and cut rest into very fine rings.

Combine lime juice, fish sauce, soy sauce, brown sugar, and ¼ cup water and whisk well. Mix in shrimp, garlic, shallots, and chiles; transfer to four small bowls. Serve dip alongside individual portions of the raw vegetable sticks.

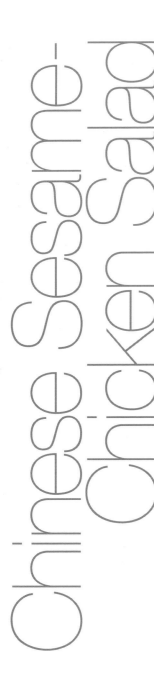

Chinese Sesame Chicken Salad

Serves 4:
Salad:
1 pound chicken breasts
1 quart chicken stock (recipe page 32 or purchased)
1 cucumber
1 fresh red Fresno chile
2 tablespoons oil
½ teaspoon crushed red pepper flakes
1 teaspoon Sichuan peppercorns
Dressing:
¼ cup sesame seeds
3 tablespoons soy sauce
2 teaspoons sesame oil
1½ tablespoons peanut oil
1 teaspoon sugar

Prep time: 30 minutes
Per serving approx: 335 calories
18 g protein/26 g fat/9 g carbohydrates

Place chicken in a pot, cover with chicken stock (plus water if needed), and bring to a boil slowly, starting with medium heat. Then cover and simmer over low heat for about 10 minutes. Pierce fillets with a knife. Chicken is cooked through when juice runs clear, not pink. Then let chicken cool in the stock.

Meanwhile, rinse cucumber, trim ends, and halve lengthwise. Scrape out seeds with a spoon and cut cucumber lengthwise into narrow strips (about 4 inches long). Rinse fresh chile, discard stem, and chop rest coarsely.

Heat oil in a pan or wok and sauté chiles and Sichuan peppercorns briefly. Add cucumber strips and sauté on high heat for about 2 minutes. Season with salt, transfer to a plate, and let cool.

Remove chicken from liquid, drain, and shred into fine strips. Arrange cucumber mixture on a platter or four plates and top with cooked chicken.

For the sauce, toast sesame seeds in a dry pan until a pale golden color. Grind in a spice mill or small food processor. Whisk together sesame seeds, soy sauce, sesame oil, peanut oil, and sugar. If the sauce is too thick, add a tiny bit of water. Drizzle over the salads and serve (either at room temperature or chilled).

Asian Slaw with Chicken

Serves 4:
¾ pound chicken breasts
Salt (preferably kosher or sea)
Freshly ground pepper
½ head small white cabbage
1 carrot
1 red Fresno chile pepper
4 green onions
2 teaspoons sugar
2 teaspoons fish sauce
1 tablespoon soy sauce
3 tablespoons lime juice
1 tablespoon rice vinegar
½ cup fresh cilantro sprigs
¼ cup fresh mint sprigs

Prep time: 35 minutes (not including cooling time)
Per serving approx: 139 calories
13 g protein/6 g fat/10 g carbohydrates

Place chicken in a pot and cover with water. Add salt and pepper and bring to a boil. Cover chicken and cook over low heat for about 10 minutes. Let cool in the liquid.

Remove any wilted leaves from cabbage, rinse, halve, core, and cut into very fine strips. Peel carrot and slice lengthwise thinly, then into shorter strips. Rinse chile, discard stem, and chop rest finely. Remove root ends and any wilted parts from green onions, rinse, cut into 1½-inch lengths, then into narrower strips.

Combine cabbage, carrot strips, chile, green onion strips, salt, and sugar, and toss together. Let vegetables stand at room temperature for about 15 minutes.

Mix fish sauce, soy sauce, lime juice, and rice vinegar. Rinse herbs, shake dry, remove tough stems, and chop rest coarsely. Drain chicken and shred into bite-size sections. Combine vegetable mixture, chicken, sauce, and herbs. Salt to taste.

Grapefruit-Shrimp Salad

Serves 4:
1 pink grapefruit
2–3 shallots
1 small cucumber
4 nice lettuce leaves
½ pound cooked peeled shrimp (small to medium), thawed
1 fresh red Fresno chile
3 tablespoons soy sauce
1 tablespoon rice vinegar
2 tablespoons lime or lemon juice
2 tablespoons honey
½ teaspoon Chinese chile-garlic sauce
Mint or cilantro leaves for sprinkling

Prep time: 25 minutes
Per serving approx: 83 calories
2 g protein/0 g fat/20 g carbohydrates

With a sharp knife, peel grapefruit so that no white membrane remains on the outside. Cut out segments from between the inner membranes. Squeeze any lingering juice out of grapefruit halves and from a few of the segments; collect in a small bowl.

Peel shallots and slice thinly. Rinse or peel cucumber, halve lengthwise, and scrape out seeds with a spoon. Cut cucumber crosswise into thin slices.

Rinse lettuce leaves, pat dry, and arrange on four plates. Top with grapefruit segments, shallots, and cucumber, plus the cooked shrimp. Rinse fresh red Fresno chile, discard stem, and chop rest. Sprinkle on salads.

Combine grapefruit juice, soy sauce, rice vinegar, citrus juice, honey, and chile sauce; drizzle over the salad. Sprinkle with herb leaves.

Ginger Beef Salad with Toasted Rice

Serves 4:
2 tablespoons medium-grain rice
1 pound beef tenderloin or ribeye
3 shallots
1 piece ginger (¾ inch)
2 cloves garlic
¼ cup fresh cilantro sprigs
4 sprigs mint
2 tablespoons oil
3 tablespoons lime juice
2 teaspoons sugar
2 teaspoons fish sauce
1 tablespoon soy sauce

Prep time: 25 minutes (not including cooling time)
Per serving approx: 442 calories
21 g protein/34 g fat/12 g carbohydrates

Heat a pan or wok on the stove. Toast rice over medium heat for about 5 minutes, until golden. Let cool, then process in a blender or food processor into very small pieces.

Freeze meat slightly and then slice very thinly. Peel shallots and slice into rings. Peel ginger and garlic and chop both finely. Rinse herbs, shake dry, remove any tough stems, and chop rest finely (reserve a few whole leaves for garnish).

Heat oil. Sauté beef over high heat for about 2 minutes while stirring well. Add rice bits, shallots, ginger, garlic, chopped herbs, lime juice, sugar, fish sauce, and soy sauce; bring to a rolling boil. Transfer salad to a bowl and let cool. Sprinkle with herb leaves as garnish.

Sweet Potato Curry

Serves 4:
2 sweet potatoes (about 1⅓ pounds)
1 leek
1 tablespoon oil
1 tablespoon green curry paste
1⅔ cups coconut milk (from a can)
½ pound cherry tomatoes
1 tablespoon lime juice
Salt (preferably kosher or sea)
Cilantro leaves for garnish

Prep time: 25 minutes
Per serving approx: 352 calories
4 g protein/30 g fat/22 g carbohydrates

Peel sweet potatoes and cut into ¾-inch cubes. Remove root end and any wilted parts from leek, slit open lengthwise, rinse thoroughly, and slice crosswise into ¼-inch-wide strips.

Heat oil in a wok or pan. Add curry paste and sauté for 1 minute. Add coconut milk and bring to a gentle boil, cooking for 1 minute. Then stir in sweet potatoes and leeks. Cover and simmer vegetables over medium heat for about 8 minutes (or until crisp-tender), checking periodically to retain liquid in pan. If insufficient, add a little water.

Rinse tomatoes and halve. Add along with lime juice to curry, and simmer for another 1–2 minutes. Salt to taste, and sprinkle with cilantro leaves.

Tofu-Vegetable Stir-Fry with Coconut Milk

Serves 4:
8 ounces firm tofu
1 medium-sized eggplant
½ pound baby spinach
1 red bell pepper
¼ pound white or Chinese cabbage
½ pound snow peas
¼ pound bean sprouts
3 shallots
1 piece ginger (¾ inch)
2 cloves garlic
1⅔ cups vegetable oil for deep-frying and frying
1⅔ cups coconut milk (from a can)
1 teaspoon ground coriander
Salt (preferably kosher or sea)

Prep time: 1 hour
Per serving approx: 447 calories
9 g protein/41 g fat/19 g carbohydrates

Cut tofu into strips about ¼-inch thick, and pat dry.

Rinse all vegetables. Cut eggplant into ¾-inch cubes. Sort spinach leaves. Cut bell pepper and cabbage into narrow strips. Leave snow peas whole. Rinse bean sprouts and drain. Peel shallots, ginger, and garlic; chop those three finely.

Heat oil to 350–375°F (use oil thermometer) in a wok or pan. Or to test for readiness, lower a wooden spoon handle into the oil. When tiny bubbles appear around it, it's hot enough. Place tofu in the oil with a metal slotted spoon and deep-fry for about 4 minutes, until golden. Remove tofu from the oil with the metal utensil and drain on a paper-towel lined plate.

Remove all but a thin coating of oil from the pan. (Pour into another pot. After cooled, you can refrigerate for later use in a bottle or container.)

Sauté the eggplant in the oil, then add the snow peas, cabbage, and bell pepper. Stir in ginger, garlic, and shallots; add bean sprouts. Pour in coconut milk, add coriander, and simmer uncovered for about 5 minutes. Stir in tofu and baby spinach, and heat until spinach wilts. Salt to taste.

Serves 4:

Condiment paste:

2 red Fresno chile peppers (mildly hot)

4 shallots

2/3 cup grated coconut (unsweetened; health food store)

1/4 teaspoon sugar

Salt (preferably kosher or sea)

Freshly ground black pepper

Soup:

1/2 pound baby spinach

1 medium-sized sweet potato (about 1/2 pound)

2 cloves garlic

1 jalapeño pepper

1 quart vegetable stock

Soy sauce for seasoning

Prep time: 35 minutes

Per serving approx: 265 calories

8 g protein/8 g fat/41 g carbohydrates

For the paste, rinse Fresno chiles and discard stems. Peel shallots. Chop both ingredients coarsely, then purée in a blender along with grated coconut and sugar to form a paste. Season to taste with salt and pepper.

For the soup, sort spinach leaves, rinse in cold water, and drain in a colander. Peel sweet potatoes, cut into slices—and then into matchsticks. Peel garlic and slice thinly. Rinse jalapeño and discard stem, seeds, and ribs; cut rest into rings (always wear gloves when working with hot peppers, and don't touch your face).

Heat stock. Add sweet potato, garlic, and jalapeño; simmer for about 5 minutes or until sweet potato is cooked through but not mushy. Add spinach; cover and simmer until the spinach wilts. Season soup with soy sauce, and serve with coconut paste as a condiment.

Curried Noodles with Oyster Mushrooms

Serves 4:
1 piece ginger (¾ inch)
4 cloves garlic
2 stalks lemon grass
2 teaspoons sambal oelek
1 teaspoon ground turmeric
1 teaspoon ground coriander
1 teaspoon ground cumin
Salt (preferably kosher or sea)
8 ounces vermicelli-sized Chinese egg noodles
1 leek
¼ pound oyster mushrooms
1 red bell pepper
8 ounces tofu
2 cups oil for deep-frying and sautéing
1⅔ cups coconut milk (from a can)
2–3 tablespoons kecap manis (sweet soy sauce)

Prep time: 40 minutes
Per serving approx: 578 calories
14 g protein/42 g fat/42 g carbohydrates

Peel ginger and garlic; mince both. Rinse lemon grass, trim ends, remove outer layer, chop coarsely, and process along with ginger and garlic in a food processor. (Or chop finely—or use a mortar and pestle.) Mix this paste with sambal oelek, turmeric, coriander, cumin, and salt.

Cook noodles in boiling water for 3–5 minutes or until cooked through but not mushy. Drain and rinse under cold water. Remove root end and any wilted parts from leek, slit open lengthwise, and rinse thoroughly. Cut into 2-inch lengths, then into narrower strips. Wipe off mushrooms with paper towels, discard stems, and slice caps. Rinse bell pepper, halve, discard stem and interior, and cut into strips.

Cut tofu into ½-inch cubes. Heat oil in a wok or pan to 350–375°F (use an oil thermometer). Pat tofu dry with paper towels, deep-fry in hot oil until golden, then remove with a metal slotted spoon. Pour oil out of the wok or pan, leaving only a thin coating. (Pour into another pan until cooled; then oil can be refrigerated in a container for later use.)

Sauté seasoning paste for 2 minutes. Add leek, bell pepper, and mushrooms; sauté for another 3–4 minutes. Pour in coconut milk and bring to a boil. Stir in noodles and tofu, and heat. Season to taste with kecap manis and salt, and serve.

Udon Noodle Soup

Serves 4:
1 leek
4 shiitake mushrooms
1 chunk daikon (about 1/3 pound)
4 ounces tofu (optional)
14 ounces udon noodles
3 cups vegetable stock
1 piece kombu (thick sheet of seaweed; Asian markets)
1/2 cup soy sauce
1 tablespoon rice wine (sake, mirin)
1 teaspoon sugar
Red radishes for garnishing
Wasabi (from a tube)
Japanese pickled ginger

Prep time: 25 minutes
Per serving approx: 477 calories
31 g protein/16 g fat/56 g carbohydrates

Remove root end and any wilted parts from leek, slit open lengthwise, rinse, and cut into strips 1/4-inch wide. Wipe off shiitake mushrooms with paper towels, discard stems, and slice caps. Peel daikon, slice thinly into rounds, and then slice into strips about 1/2-inch wide. Cut tofu diagonally into thin slices.

Cook noodles in boiling water for about 10 minutes. But don't let them get too soft! Test a noodle after 8 minutes. (If noodles are precooked, follow package instructions.)

Bring vegetable stock to a boil with kombu (break into large pieces), soy sauce, mirin, and sugar. Add leek and cook for 2 minutes. Add mushrooms and daikon and cook another 2 minutes. Remove kombu. Then add noodles and heat. Top with tofu, then with slices of red radish to garnish; ready to serve. If desired, serve wasabi and pickled ginger as accompaniments.

Indonesian Gado Gado

Serves 6:
4 medium-sized, firm potatoes
½ pound green beans
2 carrots
½ head white cabbage
⅓ pound bean sprouts
Salt (preferably kosher or sea)
1 small-sized cucumber
3 eggs (optional)
5 ounces tofu
2 onions
1 cup vegetable oil for frying
Sauce:
1 onion
3 cloves garlic
½ teaspoon crushed red pepper flakes (or to taste)
2 tablespoons oil
1⅓ cups roasted salted peanuts
1 cup coconut milk
1 tablespoon tamarind paste (from a jar) or lemon juice
¼ cup kecap manis (sweet soy sauce)

Prep time: 1½ hours
Per serving approx: 693 calories
32 g protein/51 g fat/35 g carbohydrates

Peel potatoes, rinse, and cut into ¼-inch-thick slices. Rinse beans and trim ends. Peel carrots and slice ¼-inch thick. Remove outer leaves from white cabbage. Core and slice rest into fine strips. Drain and rinse bean sprouts.

Bring a large amount of salted water to a boil for boiling vegetables: potatoes=10 minutes, beans=10 minutes, carrots=5 minutes, cabbage=2 minutes, and sprouts=1 minute. Drain and rinse each with cold water.

Peel cucumber and halve. Scrape out seeds with a spoon and slice rest finely crosswise. Hard-boil the eggs (takes 10 minutes); let cool. Cut tofu into thin slices and season with salt. Peel onions and cut into fine rings. Heat oil to 350–375°F (use oil thermometer or insert a wooden spoon handle in oil—when bubbles rise around the handle, it's ready). Fry onion slices for 6 minutes, until golden, then tofu for 3 minutes. Drain both on paper towels.

SAUCE: Peel onion and garlic; chop both finely. Sauté onion, garlic, and crushed red pepper flakes in oil. Add peanuts and coconut milk, stir well, and bring to a boil. Season to taste with tamarind paste (or lemon juice) and kecap manis. Purée in a blender; let cool. If too thick, thin with a little water.

Arrange all vegetables, sprouts, and tofu on four plates or on one large platter. Peel eggs, cut into eighths, and distribute on top along with the onion rings. Serve sauce on the side.

Seafood and Poultry

Whether it originates from the Pacific Ocean or Southeast Asia's Mekong River—or even backyard ponds—fresh fish and shellfish are undeniably a staple for Asian cooks. Their penchant for seafood, and respect for its nutritional qualities, have led to a long tradition of Asian dishes featuring aquatic life.

The varieties of seafood we have accessible to us in the United States are different from those available in Asia, but many American types make the translation—seamlessly—into Asian dishes.

Rice

One common trait found in the cooking of nearly every Asian culture is, simply, rice. Whether it be basmati, jasmine, or Japanese short-grain rice, it's the heart and soul of Asian meals. In Thailand, a common greeting of "have you eaten?" actually has a literal translation of "have you eaten rice?" And in Japan, most of the country is covered with a patchwork quilt of glassy, water-bogged rice fields—it's as important to their stomachs as it is to their bottom line.

Asian-Pesto Fish Fillets

Serves 4:

Pesto:
1 cup fresh basil sprigs
1 cup fresh mint sprigs
1 cup fresh cilantro sprigs
2 cloves garlic
1 piece ginger (¾ inch)
1 green onion
1 jalapeño pepper
⅓ cup unsalted peanuts
¼ cup peanut oil
1 pinch sugar
Salt (preferably kosher or sea)
Freshly ground black pepper
Lime juice (optional)

Fish fillets:
4 fish fillets (or 6 ounces fish for each serving; e.g., halibut, cod, monkfish, sole)
1 tablespoon lime juice
Salt (preferably kosher or sea)
Freshly ground black pepper
8–12 cherry tomatoes

Prep time: 30 minutes
Per serving approx: 272 calories
16 g protein/21 g fat/7 g carbohydrates

For the pesto, rinse herbs, shake dry, and chop leaves coarsely. Peel garlic and ginger; chop both finely. Remove root end and any wilted parts from green onion, rinse, and chop finely. Rinse jalapeño, remove stem, and chop rest finely.

Process herbs, garlic, ginger, green onion, jalapeño, and peanuts in a food processor or blender, into a paste. Add peanut oil, sugar, and a little salt—plus lime juice to taste.

For the fish, drizzle fillets with lime juice, season with salt and pepper, and place in a steamer (bamboo or metal). Rinse tomatoes, halve, and distribute over the fish.

In a large pot (the steamer must fit inside), bring about 1 cup water or vegetable stock to a boil. Place the steamer in the pot, cover, and steam fish over high heat for about 5 minutes. Transfer to pre-warmed plates and serve, along with pesto as an accompaniment. Garnish with lime wedges.

Coconut-Crusted
Spicy Fish Fillets

Serves 4:
1 shallot
2 cloves garlic
1 piece ginger (¾ inch)
1 fresh red serrano chile
2 tablespoons soy sauce
2 tablespoons rice wine (sake, mirin)
2 tablespoons lime juice
½ teaspoon ground coriander
Freshly ground black pepper
8 thin fish fillets (about 1½ pounds total; could be sole, trout, salmon)
⅔ cup grated coconut (unsweetened; health food store)
3 tablespoons oil

Prep time: 25 minutes (plus at least 2 hours marinating time)
Per serving approx: 318 calories
33 g protein/17 g fat/6 g carbohydrates

Peel shallots, garlic, and ginger; chop all three very finely. Rinse chile, discard stem, and chop very finely (omit seeds for less heat; always wear gloves when working with chiles, and don't touch your face). For the marinade, combine soy sauce, rice wine, lime juice, coriander, and pepper. Stir in shallots, garlic, ginger, and serrano.

Lay fish fillets side by side in a large dish, pour marinade over the top, and cover. Marinate fillets in the refrigerator for at least 2 hours, up to overnight. Turn occasionally if possible.

Then dredge the fish fillets in grated coconut. Heat oil in a nonstick pan and fry fillets over medium heat for 2 minutes. Turn carefully, fry the other side for 2 minutes, and they're done!

Serves 4:
1 pound firm fish fillets (e.g., swordfish, halibut, rockfish, cod, monkfish)
1 eggplant
1 small red bell pepper
1 piece ginger or galangal (¾ inch)
2 shallots
4–6 kaffir lime leaves (Asian market)
2 tablespoons oil
2 tablespoons green curry paste
1⅔ cups coconut milk (from a can)
1 tablespoon brown sugar
1 tablespoon fish sauce
Several sprigs basil (Thai basil if available)

Prep time: 35 minutes
Per serving approx: 418 calories
9 g protein/36 g fat/20 g carbohydrates

With your fingers, feel the fish for bones—use tweezers to remove any you find. Cut fillets into 1-inch cubes or a little larger if desired. Rinse eggplant, discard stem, and cut rest into small cubes. Rinse bell pepper, halve, remove contents, discard stem, and cut rest into diamond shapes.

Peel ginger or galangal, and slice thinly. Peel shallots, halve, and cut into strips. Rinse lime leaves and tear into pieces.

Heat oil in a wok or pan and brown ginger or galangal and shallots. Stir in curry paste and sauté for 1 minute. Add coconut milk, lime leaves, brown sugar, and fish sauce; simmer for about 5 minutes. The lime leaves should be releasing their aroma.

Stir in eggplant and bell pepper, cooking for 4 more minutes. Add fish, reduce heat slightly, and cook for another 3 minutes or until fish is cooked through.

Remove leaves from basil stems and brush off with a paper towel, if necessary. Stir leaves into curry, salt to taste, and serve. Goes great with hot cooked rice.

Japanese Mixed Tempura

Serves 4:
1 pound firm-type fish fillets (e.g., swordfish, rockfish, cod, monkfish)
⅓ pound uncooked shrimp (peeled and deveined)
8 shiitake mushrooms
1 pound asparagus spears (or green beans)
6 green onions
½ small head napa (Chinese) cabbage
1 quart vegetable oil for deep-frying

Batter:
¾ cup flour
1 egg

Dip:
1 chunk daikon radish (about 2 inches)
1 piece ginger (¾ inch)
½ cup soy sauce
½ cup mirin (sweet Japanese rice wine)
¼ cup sake (Japanese rice wine)

Prep time: 1 hour
Per serving approx: 472 calories
30 g protein/20 g fat/31 g carbohydrates

Rinse fish and pat dry with paper towels. Thaw, rinse, and pat dry shrimp.

Wipe off mushrooms with paper towels. Discard stems. Rinse asparagus, trim ends, and cut into ¾-inch lengths. Remove root ends and any wilted parts from green onions, rinse, and cut into ¾-inch sections. Rinse Chinese cabbage leaves, pat dry, and cut into strips.

For the batter, whisk flour, egg, and ¾ cup plus 2 tablespoons ice-cold water together.

For the dip, peel daikon and ginger; grate both. Briefly bring to a boil soy sauce, mirin, and sake; let cool. Stir in daikon and ginger; transfer dip to individual small bowls.

In a wok or pan, heat oil for deep-frying. Set oven to 170°F and warm a large, oven-safe platter.

When the oil is hot (use an oil thermometer, 350–375°F), first dip fish, then shrimp, and then vegetables in batter; immediately place in the hot oil using a metal utensil. Don't add too much at once or the oil will not keep the proper temperature. When golden, remove pieces with a metal utensil and transfer to the warmed platter (lined with paper towels). Keep warm in the oven.

Finish all the batches, and serve dip alongside tempura.

Tuna in Miso Marinade

Serves 4:

4 tuna steaks (about 6 ounces each; or substitute other types of fish)
3 tablespoons miso
¼ cup mirin (sweet Japanese rice wine)
3 tablespoons sake (Japanese rice wine)
1 tablespoon soy sauce
2 tablespoons vegetable oil (if needed)

Prep time: 15 minutes (plus 4 hours marinating time)
Per serving approx: 216 calories
17 g protein/11 g fat/5 g carbohydrates

Rinse and pat dry fish; place in a bowl. Stir together miso, mirin, sake, and soy sauce; pour marinade over the fish, cover, and marinate for at least 4 hours, refrigerated. Turn the fish once halfway through.

Afterwards you can either grill or sauté the fish. If you want to grill it, turn on the charcoal grill or oven broiler. Then either broil the fillets or grill for about 3–4 minutes per side or until cooked through.

If you wish to sauté, heat oil and cook fish over medium heat for about 5 minutes on each side.

Five-Spice Fish Fillets

Serves 4 (light entrée or appetizer):
1 pound thin fish fillets (e.g., trout, sole, snapper)
¼ cup rice wine (sake, mirin)
Salt (preferably kosher or sea)
1 piece ginger (about ½ inch)
4 cloves garlic
2 tablespoons vegetable oil
2 tablespoons soy sauce
1 teaspoon sugar
1 teaspoon five-spice powder
5 green onions
1 teaspoon sesame oil

Prep time: 1¼ hours
Per serving approx: 147 calories
9 g protein/8 g fat/5 g carbohydrates

Check the fish fillets for bones and remove any you find with tweezers. Then cut fillets into bite-size pieces. Combine rice wine with a little salt and distribute evenly on all sides of the fish. Cover and marinate in the refrigerator for at least 30 minutes.

Peel ginger and garlic; chop both finely. Heat oil in a pan or wok. Sauté fish pieces very briefly (to sear) and remove from oil (these will be cooked more later). Sauté garlic and ginger in this same oil. Add 1 cup water, soy sauce, sugar, and five-spice powder, and bring to a boil. Place fish in this liquid, reduce heat, and simmer uncovered for about 10 minutes.

Meanwhile, trim root ends and any wilted parts from green onions, rinse, and slice into fine rings. Remove fish from cooking liquid and transfer to individual plates (warm plates first in a 170°F oven). Ladle some cooking liquid over the top, sprinkle with green onions, and drizzle with sesame oil to serve.

Sweet and Tangy Shrimp

Serves 4:
1¼ pounds uncooked shrimp (small-sized, peeled and de-veined)
2 tablespoons rice wine (sake, mirin)
2 tablespoons lime juice
2 cloves garlic
1 onion
2–3 stalks celery
2 tomatoes
3 tablespoons vegetable oil
1 tablespoon brown sugar
2 teaspoons fish sauce
1 tablespoon soy sauce
1 teaspoon cornstarch
1 tablespoon ketchup
Salt (preferably kosher or sea)
Cilantro leaves for garnish

Prep time: 25 minutes
Per serving approx: 307 calories
30 g protein/13 g fat/14 g carbohydrates

Thaw, rinse, and pat dry shrimp. Mix with 1 tablespoon of the rice wine and 1 tablespoon of the lime juice.

Peel garlic and onion. Slice garlic thinly. Halve onion and slice into strips. Rinse celery, trim ends, and slice rest thinly. Rinse tomatoes, core, and dice.

Heat oil in a wok or pan and briefly sauté celery, garlic, and onion. Add shrimp and sauté for another minute.

Add remaining rice wine, lime juice, brown sugar, fish sauce, soy sauce, ketchup, and tomatoes; simmer for 2–3 minutes. Mix cornstarch into ⅓ cup water, add to pan, and bring to a boil. Salt to taste, sprinkle with cilantro, and enjoy. Serve with hot cooked rice.

Serves 4 as a light entrée or appetizer:
2¼ pounds clams
1 piece ginger (¾ inch)
1 clove garlic
2 green onions
1 tablespoon vegetable oil
1 cup sake (Japanese rice wine)
3 tablespoons soy sauce
1 teaspoon sugar

Prep time: 30 minutes
Per serving approx: 211 calories
16 g protein/5 g fat/10 g carbohydrates

Rinse clams thoroughly under cold running water. If they're very dirty, scrub with a brush. Make sure the clams close when you rinse them—toss any that don't.

Peel ginger and garlic, cut into paper-thin slices—and then into very fine strips. Remove root ends and any wilted parts from green onions, rinse, and slice thinly into rings.

Heat oil in a large pot or in a wok. Briefly sauté ginger, garlic, and green onions. Add sake, soy sauce, and sugar; bring to a boil. Then add clams and cover immediately. Cook clams over high heat for 3–5 minutes until they open. If after 5 minutes most remain closed, cook covered for a little longer and check again.

IMPORTANT: Throw away any clams that don't open. Serve clams along with cooking liquid.

Indian Curried Chicken and Rice

Serves 4:
1⅓ cups basmati rice
1 pound chicken breasts
2 onions
1 piece ginger (¾ inch)
1 green bell pepper
2 tomatoes
3 tablespoons clarified butter or ghee (specialty grocery store, or make by melting butter—skim and discard any solids that rise to the surface)
1 cinnamon stick
4 whole cloves
4 whole green cardamom pods
2 teaspoons curry powder (or 1 teaspoon turmeric and 1 teaspoon Hungarian paprika)
¼ cup yogurt
Salt (preferably kosher or sea)
2 tablespoons raisins
2 tablespoons sliced almonds

Prep time: 40 minutes
Per serving approx: 568 calories
28 g protein/23 g fat/66 g carbohydrates

Rinse rice using a fine mesh strainer until water runs clear. Drain well. Cut chicken breasts into bite-size cubes.

Peel onions and dice. Peel ginger and grate. Rinse and halve bell pepper. Discard seeds, ribs, and stem; dice rest finely. Core tomatoes and cover with boiling water in a bowl; let stand briefly, rinse with cold water, and slip off peels; then dice.

In a pot, heat 1 tablespoon of the clarified butter. Sauté diced chicken until golden on all sides; remove. Melt another tablespoon of the butter and sauté cinnamon stick, cloves, cardamom pods, and curry powder for 1 minute.

Add onions, ginger, and bell pepper—sauté briefly. Add rice and stir to mix well. Stir in tomatoes, yogurt, and 2 cups warm water. Cover and simmer over low heat for about 15 minutes.

Add chicken and raisins, and cook for another 5 minutes or until the rice is al dente.

Meanwhile, melt remaining clarified butter in a small pan. Stir in sliced almonds and sauté until golden. Salt the curried chicken and rice to taste (remove cloves, cinnamon stick, and cardamom pods). Garnish with toasted almonds.

Serves 4:
1¼ cups jasmine rice
1 piece ginger (¾ inch)
1 stalk lemon grass
2 cups chicken stock
4 whole cloves
1 teaspoon sambal oelek
½ teaspoon ground turmeric
1 teaspoon ground cumin
1 pinch ground cinnamon
2 eggs
Salt (preferably kosher or sea)
3 tablespoons vegetable oil
1 red bell pepper
1 green bell pepper
⅓ pound cooked ham
⅓ pound peeled cooked shrimp, rinsed and thawed
3 tablespoons kecap manis (sweet soy sauce, Asian grocery)

Prep time: 40 minutes
Per serving approx: 503 calories
23 g protein/19 g fat/58 g carbohydrates

Using a fine mesh strainer, rinse rice well and drain.

Peel ginger and slice thinly. Rinse lemon grass, remove outer layer, trim ends, and cut rest into ¾-inch sections. In a pot, combine: ginger, lemon grass, chicken stock, cloves, sambal oelek, turmeric, cumin, and cinnamon. Add rice, bring to a boil, cover, reduce heat, and simmer for about 20 minutes. Then, remove lemon grass and cloves.

Meanwhile, whisk eggs and 1–2 tablespoons water thoroughly; salt lightly. In a nonstick pan, heat 1 tablespoon of the oil. Pour in egg mixture, spread around thinly and cook on medium-low until it sets. Flip, cook bottom briefly, and remove from pan; let cool.

Rinse and halve bell peppers. Remove seeds and ribs, discard stems, and cut rest into narrow strips. Finely dice ham.

Heat remaining oil and sauté ham and peppers until pepper strips are al dente. Add ham, peppers, shrimp, and kecap manis to cooked rice; stir. Salt to taste. Cut omelet into narrow strips and fold into rice mixture. Cover pan and heat briefly, until egg and shrimp are heated through.

Chile-Garlic Fried Noodles

Serves 4
8 ounces vermicelli-sized Chinese egg noodles
2 stalks lemon grass
3 fresh red Fresno chiles (mildly spicy)
2 cloves garlic
1 shallot
1 piece ginger (¾ inch)
⅓ pound chicken breast
2 tablespoons soy sauce
8 ounces spinach
⅓ pound bean sprouts
1 small cucumber
5–6 tablespoons oil
Salt (preferably kosher or sea)
Crushed red pepper flakes, to taste
Mint and/or basil leaves for sprinkling

Prep time: 40 minutes
Per serving approx: 483 calories
19 g protein/23 g fat/54 g carbohydrates

Add noodles to a large pot of boiling, salted water. Immediately remove pot from heat and let noodles soak for 4 minutes. Then drain and rinse well under cold water.

Rinse lemon grass, trim ends, remove outer later, and mince rest. Rinse chiles, discard stems, and mince rest finely. Peel and mince garlic, shallot, and ginger. Mix these three with chiles and lemon grass—mince together to create a seasoning paste.

Cut chicken into thin strips and mix with soy sauce. Rinse spinach well, drain, discard any thick stems, and tear any large leaves into smaller pieces. Rinse and drain bean sprouts. Rinse cucumber, halve lengthwise, scrape out seeds with a spoon, and slice the rest thinly crosswise.

Heat oil in a nonstick pan. Stir-fry cooked noodles briefly, then remove. Add chicken and bean sprouts; stir. Add cucumber and sauté briefly. Stir in seasoning paste and sauté for 1 minute. Add spinach, and stir, until it wilts. Then add noodles; salt to taste. If you desire more heat, add crushed red pepper flakes to taste. Sprinkle with mint and/or basil, and serve.

Serves 4:
1⅓ pounds chicken breasts
1 egg white
1 tablespoon cornstarch
Salt (preferably kosher or sea)
1–2 red bell peppers
5 green onions
2 cloves garlic
4-6 fresh red Fresno chiles
3 tablespoons soy sauce
2 tablespoons rice wine (sake, mirin)
2 tablespoons rice vinegar
2 teaspoons sugar
1 teaspoon sesame oil
⅓ cup vegetable oil
⅔ cup cashews

Prep time: 20 minutes
Per serving approx: 580 calories
32 g protein/32 g fat/21 g carbohydrates

Cut chicken breasts into ½-inch cubes. Mix with egg white, cornstarch, and salt.

Rinse bell peppers, halve, and discard stems, ribs, and seeds; cut rest into strips. Remove root ends and any dark green or wilted parts from green onions, rinse, and slice rest into thin rings. Peel garlic. Rinse chiles and discard stems. Finely mince garlic and chiles together (wear gloves and don't touch your face). Combine soy sauce, rice wine, rice vinegar, sugar, and sesame oil in a small bowl.

Heat wok or pan, pour in oil, and sauté cashews for about 1 minute until golden. Remove with a slotted metal spoon, drain well, and set aside.

Add bell peppers, green onions, and the garlic-chile mixture to the hot oil—sauté over high heat for 1 minute. Stir in chicken and stir-fry for about 2 minutes or longer, until cooked through. Pour in sauce, add cashews, heat well, and it's ready! Pairs well with hot cooked rice.

Walnut Chicken

Serves 4:
1⅓ pounds chicken breasts
2 teaspoons cornstarch
¼ cup rice wine (sake, mirin)
5 green onions
1 piece ginger (¾ inch)
⅔ cup walnuts
¼ cup vegetable oil
3–4 tablespoons soy sauce

Prep time: 20 minutes
Per serving approx: 494 calories
31 g protein/37 g fat/7 g carbohydrates

Cut chicken breasts into ¾-inch cubes. Stir cornstarch into 2 tablespoons of the rice wine and mix well with chicken cubes.

Remove root ends and any dark green or wilted parts from green onions, and rinse rest; cut into ¾-inch lengths. Peel ginger, slice thinly, and then slice into matchsticks. Break walnuts into small pieces or chop coarsely.

Heat oil in a wok or pan, add walnuts, and stir-fry for 1–2 minutes or until golden. Remove and set aside.

Add chicken to the pan and stir-fry for 1 minute. Add onions and ginger and stir-fry for another minute. Combine remaining rice wine, soy sauce, and about ⅓ cup water and add to chicken along with walnuts. Stir-fry for another minute, make sure chicken is cooked through, and serve. Great with hot cooked rice.

Serves 4:
1¾ pound chicken breasts
Juice from 2 lemons
Drops red food coloring
Salt (preferably kosher or sea)
1 piece ginger (¾ inch)
3 cloves garlic
1 teaspoon each of ground cumin, ground coriander, ground turmeric, Hungarian paprika,
and freshly grated nutmeg
½ teaspoon chili powder
½ teaspoon freshly ground black pepper
1¾ cups yogurt

Prep time: 15 minutes
(plus marinating time of 30 minutes and overnight plus 35 minutes roasting time)
Per serving approx: 359 calories
38 g protein/19 g fat/11 g carbohydrates

Make slits in chicken breasts about ⅛-inch deep, spaced ¾-inch apart. Place in a bowl. Combine lemon juice and many drops of food coloring; pour over chicken breasts. It should look very red. Season with salt, and let stand for about 30 minutes.

Peel ginger and garlic. Squeeze both through a press and stir into yogurt along with all the other spices. Pour sauce over chicken, mix well, cover, and marinate overnight (refrigerated).

On the next day, preheat oven to 350°F. Cover a baking sheet with aluminum foil. Remove chicken breasts from marinade, arrange side by side on the baking sheet, and roast in the oven (middle rack) for about 35 minutes (reserve marinade). Halfway through and then once more before finished, turn chicken and brush with more marinade.

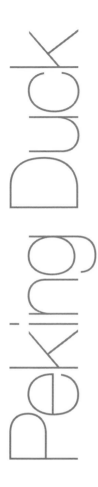

Peking Duck

Serves 4:

Duck:
2 duck breasts with skin (about 12 ounces each)
2 tablespoons molasses
1 heaping teaspoon salt (preferably kosher or sea)

Pancakes:
2 cups flour, plus more for working the dough
Sesame oil and vegetable oil for frying

Accompaniments:
10 green onions
1 small cucumber
$\frac{1}{4}$ cup red bean paste (Asian grocery)
2 teaspoons sesame oil
Plum sauce (bottled, Asian grocery)

Prep time: 1 hour (plus about 8 hours marinating)
Per serving approx: 474 calories
19 g protein/13 g fat/69 g carbohydrates

DUCK BREASTS (SKIN-ON): About 8 hours ahead of time, boil molasses in $\frac{1}{3}$ cup salted water. Place breasts in a bowl, cover with molasses mixture, and let stand 15 minutes. Drain duck but reserve the syrup; let dry with skin side up for about 1 hour. Spread with syrup and let stand for 7 hours (5 of which should be refrigerated).

PANCAKES: Knead together flour and $\frac{1}{2}$ cup lukewarm water and wrap in a damp non-terry dishtowel. Let stand 20 minutes.

DUCK BREASTS: Preheat oven to 375°F. Roast duck on middle rack with skin side up for 30 minutes, until skin is crispy (then reduce heat to 170°F).

Meanwhile, remove root ends and any wilted parts from green onions, rinse, cut into 2-inch lengths—then cut into thin strips. Rinse cucumber, halve lengthwise, scrape out seeds, and slice rest crosswise thinly.

PANCAKES: Knead the dough once more and divide into 20 pieces. Roll each piece first into a ball and then into thin rounds on a floured workspace. Brush a hot non-stick pan with a little sesame and vegetable oils; cook the pancakes one at a time for 1 minute per side. Wrap pancakes in a slightly damp cloth; place in warm oven.

TO SERVE: Remove duck breasts from oven; slice very finely. Return to warm oven until serving time. For the sauce, mix bean paste and sesame oil. Pour into individual bowls for serving (likewise with the plum sauce, onion strips, and cucumber slices).

Transfer duck slices to small plates and serve alongside pancakes. Each guest can: spread a thin layer of one of the sauces on a pancake, top with duck, sprinkle with cucumber or green onions, and roll it up.

Beef, Pork, and Lamb

Broaching the subject of meat in Asia is a bit like opening Pandora's box. For religious reasons, some groups avoid beef, while others avoid pork. For financial reasons, many in poorer Asian villages avoid cooking with pricey proteins altogether—for them, meat is a true luxury.

Nevertheless, there is no single stereotype that can apply to the whole of Asia's meat consumption. A lengthy tradition of meat-based classics has risen out of the continent—as surely it will continue, with a future of more innovative beef, pork, and lamb dishes to come.

Noodles

Although perhaps not as integral as rice, noodles certainly hold their own in Asian cooking. With varied sizes and compositions—from vermicelli-sized Chinese egg noodles, to fettuccine-like rice noodles, to fat Japanese wheat udon noodles—their versatility is unmatched. One Japanese custom of eating buckwheat-based Soba noodles on New Year's Eve even purports that the noodles' length symbolizes a long and happy life for all who partake.

Japanese Sukiyaki

Serves 6:
1½ pounds beef tenderloin, filet, or ribeye
3½ ounces cellophane noodles
8 ounces tofu
1 small head napa (Chinese) cabbage
2 cups spinach
2 small leeks (or 6 green onions)
⅓ pound shiitake mushrooms
4 very fresh eggs (optional), or pasteurized eggs
¼ cup vegetable oil
Sauce:
½ cup dashi stock (page 32, or instant dashi, or chicken stock)
½ cup soy sauce
½ cup rice wine (sake, mirin)
2 tablespoons sugar

Prep time: 35 minutes
Per serving approx: 688 calories
32 g protein/41 g fat/46 g carbohydrates

(Make some rice for eating with the sukiyaki.) Prepare ingredients ahead of time for cooking at the table: freeze beef for one hour, then slice thinly. Cover cellophane noodles with water until soft; drain. Cut tofu into ¾-inch cubes. Rinse napa cabbage and cut into 1-inch strips. Rinse spinach well, drain, and discard any tough stems. Clean leeks, halve lengthwise, rinse well, and slice crosswise thinly. Wipe off shiitake mushrooms with paper towels, discard stems, and slice caps. Arrange ingredients on platters.

SAUCE: Bring to a boil dashi, soy sauce, rice wine, and sugar: pour into a pitcher or glass measuring cup. Whisk the eggs and portion out to four individual bowls for each place setting. (Do not serve to young children or to the elderly, unless pasteurized eggs, as eggs will be consumed partially raw.)

Use a gas or electric burner on the table, with a sturdy, low-sided pan (or use fondue pot). Heat oil in pot at the table. First brown a little meat that has been drizzled with a small amount of sauce. Then add tofu and vegetables, then a few glass noodles and, finally, a little sauce. After a few minutes, the first ingredients are ready for the taking. Dip cooked items in egg briefly (if desired), then eat with rice. Keep adding ingredients and sauce to the pot.

Spicy Lemon Grass Beef

Serves 4:
1½ pounds beef tenderloin, filet, ribeye, or New York strip
1 tablespoon soy sauce
1 teaspoon fish sauce
2 stalks lemon grass
4 cloves garlic
1 piece ginger (¾ inch)
3 fresh red Fresno chiles
5 green onions
⅔ pound tomatoes
¼ cup vegetable oil
½ cup Asian chicken stock (page 32) or purchased
1 teaspoon sugar
1 tablespoon kecap manis (sweet soy sauce, Asian grocery)
Salt (preferably kosher or sea)
Cilantro leaves for garnish

Prep time: 25 minutes
Per serving approx: 659 calories
33 g protein/53 g fat/12 g carbohydrates

Using a sharp knife, slice beef as thinly as possible against the grain. Then cut slices into bite-size pieces. Combine meat with soy and fish sauces.

Rinse lemon grass, trim ends, remove outer layer, and finely chop rest. Peel garlic and ginger; chop both. Process lemon grass, garlic, and ginger in a small food processor or blender (add a bit of water if necessary)—or mince together finely.

Rinse chiles, discard stems, and slice rest finely into rings. Remove root ends and any wilted parts from green onions, rinse, and cut into 1½-inch lengths; then halve these pieces lengthwise. Core and rinse tomatoes, then dice.

Heat oil in a wok or large pan and stir-fry meat for 2 minutes. Remove and add onions and chiles; sauté for 1 minute. Stir in lemon grass paste and tomatoes. Pour in stock, sugar, and kecap manis. Return meat to pan (to warm through), and increase heat. Salt to taste, garnish with cilantro, and serve.

Sesame Eggplant with Beef

Serves 4:
2 small-sized eggplants (about 7 ounces each)
⅓ pound shiitake or oyster mushrooms
½ pound beef tenderloin or filet
4 shallots
4 cloves garlic
1 piece ginger (¾ inch)
1 tablespoon fermented black beans (Chinese grocery)
3½ tablespoons sesame seeds
⅓ cup vegetable oil
3 tablespoons rice wine (sake, mirin)
3 tablespoons soy sauce
1–2 teaspoons sambal oelek
1 pinch ground cinnamon
Salt (preferably kosher or sea)
1 teaspoon cornstarch
1 teaspoon sesame oil

Prep time: 35 minutes
Per serving approx: 551 calories
17 g protein/37 g fat/41 g carbohydrates

Rinse eggplants and trim stems. Quarter lengthwise, then slice those thinly crosswise. Discard mushroom stems, then wipe off and slice caps. Cut beef into thin slices against the grain, and then into bite-size strips.

Peel shallots and slice thinly. Peel garlic and ginger; mince both. Chop black beans coarsely.

Heat a wok or pan. Toast sesame seeds in a dry pan until golden, stirring (then remove). Pour in 2 tablespoons of the oil, brown the beef, and remove. Pour in rest of oil, heat, and brown eggplant on all sides while stirring constantly. Add mushrooms and stir-fry for 2–3 minutes.

Add shallots, garlic, ginger, black beans, beef, and sesame seeds to the wok or pan. Stir together soy sauce, sambal oelek , and ⅓ cup water—add. Season with cinnamon and cook, uncovered, 3–4 minutes.

Stir cornstarch into a little cold water, stir into vegetables, and return to a boil. Salt to taste, drizzle with sesame oil, and serve.

Serves 4:
8 ounces wide rice noodles
1 pound beef tenderloin, filet, or ribeye
1 pound bok choy (2 medium heads; or substitute broccoli)
2 onions
4 cloves garlic
⅓ cup vegetable oil
3 tablespoons oyster sauce
2 teaspoons fish sauce
1 tablespoon sugar
Salt (preferably kosher or sea), if needed
Condiments:
⅔ cup roasted salted peanuts, chopped
Chili powder
Rice vinegar
Cilantro leaves

Prep time: 30 minutes
Per serving approx: 881 calories
29 g protein/57 g fat/65 g carbohydrates

Cook noodles in boiling water for about 4 minutes; rinse and drain.

Cut beef into thin slices and then into wide strips. Rinse bok choy, halve lengthwise, and then cut crosswise into wide strips. Precook bok choy in boiling, salted water for 2 minutes, then remove and drain. Peel onions, halve, and then cut into wide strips. Peel garlic and slice thinly.

Heat oil in a wok or large pan and sauté garlic, onions, and beef for about 2 minutes. Add bok choy and sauté another 2 minutes.

Add noodles, oyster sauce, fish sauce, and sugar; heat thoroughly while stirring constantly. Add salt to taste.

Serve with the following alongside as condiments (guests can pick and choose): peanuts, chili powder, vinegar, cilantro.

Sweet and Sour Pork

Serves 4:
1½ pounds lean pork
2 tablespoons cornstarch
2 tablespoons rice wine
1 egg
Salt (preferably kosher or sea)
1 red bell pepper
½ cucumber (or 4-inch section)
1 leek
1 piece ginger (¾ inch)
2 cloves garlic
3 tablespoons sugar
3 tablespoons rice vinegar
2 tablespoons rice wine (sake, mirin)
2 tablespoons soy sauce
2 tablespoons tomato purée or ketchup
2½ cups oil for deep-frying

Prep time: 35 minutes
Per serving approx: 496 calories
39 g protein/25 g fat/24 g carbohydrates

Cut pork into ½-inch slices, then into ½-inch strips. Whisk together: cornstarch, rice wine, egg, and 1 pinch salt. Combine mixture and pork well (this will form the batter/coating).

Rinse bell pepper, halve lengthwise, and discard stem, seeds, and ribs. Cut into diamonds, squares, or rectangles. Rinse cucumber piece, halve lengthwise, scrape out seeds, and slice crosswise thinly. Remove root end and any wilted or dark green parts from leek, slit open lengthwise, rinse well, and slice crosswise thinly. Peel ginger and garlic; mince both.

Mix together well: sugar, rice vinegar, rice wine, soy sauce, and tomato purée or ketchup.

Warm an oven-safe platter in a 170°F oven (line platter with paper towels). Heat oil in a hot wok or deep pot (to 350–375°F using an oil thermometer). Deep-fry pork strips in batches—about 3 minutes each. Remove with a slotted metal spoon, transfer to platter, and keep warm in oven.

After the last batch, pour all the oil out of the pan except for a thin coating (pour it into another pot, let it cool, then strain it and pour into a container for future use). Sauté bell pepper in pan for 1 minute. Add leek, cucumber, ginger, and garlic, and sauté another minute. Pour in sauce and heat. Quickly mix with the pork and serve immediately so strips stay crispy. Pairs great with hot cooked rice.

Chinese Ma Po Tofu

Serves 4:
1 piece ginger (¾ inch)
2 green onions
4 cloves garlic
16 ounces firm tofu
3 tablespoons oil
½ pound ground pork (or beef)
2–3 tablespoons black bean sauce (Asian grocery)
About 1 cup chicken stock (page 32 or purchased)
Soy sauce for seasoning
Sesame oil for drizzling
Chili oil for drizzling

Prep time: 20 minutes
Per serving approx: 466 calories
29 g protein/37 g fat/8 g carbohydrates

Peel ginger and grate. Remove root end and wilted parts from green onions, rinse, and cut into rings. Peel garlic and mince. Cut tofu into ½-inch cubes

In a wok or pan, heat oil and briefly sauté ginger, green onions, and garlic. Add ground meat and stir-fry until lightly browned and crumbly.

Spoon bean sauce into the wok or pan and stir. Pour in stock and heat. Then add tofu to the sauce, reduce heat, and simmer for about 5 minutes. Season to taste with soy sauce. Serve, with sesame and chili oils alongside as condiments. Hot cooked rice is a perfect accompaniment.

Pork in Spicy Caramel Sauce

Serves 4:

1½ pounds pork for stewing (e.g., shoulder; ask butcher)
1⅔ cups chicken stock (page 32 or purchased)
3 chile peppers (mixture of red Fresnos and jalapeños)
1 piece ginger (¾ inch)
3 tablespoons brown sugar
¼ cup oil
1 tablespoon fish sauce
2 tablespoons lime juice

Prep time: 2 hours
Per serving approx: 314 calories
20 g protein/20 g fat/12 g carbohydrates

ADD TO POT: pork, chicken stock, and 2 cups water; bring to a boil. Cover and simmer over low heat for 1½ to 2 hours. (liquid should look like it's just about to boil, but not be rapidly boiling). Meat should be tender; if not, cook a little longer. Let cool in the liquid.

Then remove pork (reserve liquid). Slice thinly, and then cut it into strips. Rinse chiles, discard stems, and cut rest into strips (wear gloves when working with hot peppers, and don't touch your face). Peel ginger, cut into paper-thin slices, and then into strips.

In a small pan, heat brown sugar and ½ cup of the reserved cooking liquid until the sugar dissolves. Add chiles and ginger, and simmer briefly.

Heat oil in a wok or pan and fry meat strips in batches (about 4) until browned, then remove. After the last batch, return all to the wok and add the brown sugar sauce. Season to taste with fish sauce, lime juice, and salt; bring to a boil. Serve with hot cooked rice.

Deep-Fried Pork Ribs with Napa Cabbage

Serves 4:

Ribs:

1 large piece ginger (about 2 inches)
4 cloves garlic
3 tablespoons honey
2 teaspoons sesame oil
¼ cup soy sauce
½ cup black bean sauce
3½ pounds meaty spareribs
4 cups oil for deep-frying

Napa cabbage:

1 small head napa (Chinese) cabbage
1 large onion
2 tablespoons oil
½ cup chicken (page 32) or vegetable stock (purchased okay)
2 tablespoons soy sauce
2 tablespoons rice vinegar
1 tablespoon sambal oelek or Chinese chile-garlic sauce

Prep time: 30 minutes (plus at least 12 hours marinating time)
Per serving approx: 724 calories
27 g protein/58 g fat/24 g carbohydrates

Peel ginger and garlic; squeeze both through a press. Mix with honey, sesame oil, soy sauce, and black bean sauce. Rinse spareribs, pat dry, and cut apart individual ribs. Brush generously with marinade, cover, and refrigerate for 12 hours.

JUST BEFORE COOKING THE RIBS: Rinse napa cabbage well and cut into 3/4-inch strips. Peel onion, halve, and cut into strips. Heat oil in a pan and sauté onion for 2 minutes. Add napa cabbage and sauté briefly. Add stock, soy sauce, rice vinegar, and sambal oelek. Cover and simmer over very low heat until cabbage is tender and tasty.

Heat oil for deep-frying in a wok or pot (to 350–375°F, using an oil thermometer). Or, test by sticking the handle of a wooden spoon in the oil; when a lot of tiny bubbles congregate around it, the oil is hot enough. Reduce heat to medium. Fry the ribs in the oil in batches, for 6 minutes. Remove with a metal slotted spoon and fry the next batch likewise.

Transfer the fried ribs to a platter lined with paper towels—place in a 170°F oven to keep warm.

When the ribs are ready, salt napa cabbage mixture to taste, and serve alongside ribs.

Serves 4:
½ pound ground pork
2 tablespoons rice wine
2 stalks celery
1 small red bell pepper
1 carrot
1 piece ginger (¾ inch)
4 cloves garlic
2 tablespoons oil plus 3 cups for deep-frying
2 tablespoons black bean sauce (Asian grocery)
¼ cup soy sauce
5 ounces cellophane noodles

Prep time: 25 minutes
Per serving approx: 507 calories
12 g protein/33 g fat/39 g carbohydrates

Mix ground pork with rice wine; let stand. Rinse celery and bell pepper. Peel carrot. Halve bell pepper and discard stem, seeds, and ribs. Dice all vegetables finely. Peel ginger and garlic; mince both.

Heat 2 tablespoons oil in a wok or pan and sauté ginger and garlic. Add vegetables and stir-fry for 2 minutes. Then add pork and cook until it becomes crumbly. (Break apart the meat while stirring.)

Now add black bean sauce, soy sauce, and ½ cup water; stir and keep sauce hot.

Heat oil for frying; to test, insert a wooden spoon handle into the oil. When a lot of bubbles congregate around it, it's hot enough. Divide the cellophane noodles into two or three portions, untangle them a little, and drop them into the oil one batch at a time. When the noodles puff up and turn snow-white, remove from oil with a metal slotted spoon. After the last batch, transfer fried noodles to individual bowls, cover with meat sauce, and serve immediately.

Rice Noodles and Spicy Pork

Serves 4:
1½ pounds pork loin or tenderloin
⅓ cup sugar
1 tablespoon fish sauce
1 tablespoon soy sauce
8 ounces fine rice noodles
6 green onions
¾ cup fresh mint sprigs
¾ cup fresh basil sprigs
1 bunch cilantro
1 cucumber
½ pound bean sprouts
⅔ cup roasted salted peanuts, chopped
2 tablespoons oil
Dip:
2 fresh red Fresno chiles
2 cloves garlic
¼ cup soy sauce
1 tablespoon fish sauce
3 tablespoons lime juice

Prep time: 40 minutes
Per serving approx: 628 calories
41 g protein/15 g fat/83 g carbohydrates

Cut pork into bite-size strips. Melt sugar in a pot while stirring until golden. Add fish sauce and soy sauce; bring to a boil. Combine this mixture with pork strips; let stand. Place rice noodles in a bowl, cover with lukewarm water, and soak for 20 minutes.

Remove root ends and any wilted parts from green onions, rinse, and cut into fine rings. Rinse herbs, shake dry, and discard any tough stems. Rinse cucumber, halve lengthwise, remove seeds, and slice rest thinly into sticks. Cook bean sprouts in salted, boiling water for 1 minute, then drain. Divide green onions, cucumber, bean sprouts, and peanuts amongst four dinner plates (for serving).

DIP: Rinse chiles, discard stems, and chop rest finely. Peel garlic and mince. Mix chiles, garlic, soy sauce, fish sauce, and lime juice; transfer to four individual bowls. Drain noodles and distribute on the dinner plates. Place dip alongside.

Heat oil in a wok or pan and brown pork over high heat in 2 batches for about 2 minutes each. When the second batch is done, return the first batch to the pan and heat. Distribute meat near the noodles on the plates. Guests can mix ingredients together to enjoy.

Indian Lamb with Eggplant and Lentils

Serves 4:
1 pound lamb (e.g., leg, lean shoulder, or breast without bone)
1 eggplant
2 onions
1 piece ginger (¾ inch)
2 fresh red Fresno chiles
4 tomatoes
¼ cup clarified butter or ghee (specialty store, or make your own by melting butter and skimming and discarding any white solids that rise to the surface)
1 teaspoon ground turmeric
1 teaspoon Hungarian paprika
1 teaspoon ground cumin
¾ cup red lentils
1 tablespoon lemon juice
1 teaspoon sugar
Salt (preferably kosher or sea)
Garam masala for sprinkling

Prep time: 30 minutes (plus 1 hour stewing time)
Per serving approx: 554 calories
29 g protein/32 g fat/43 g carbohydrates

Cut lamb into 1-inch cubes, trimming away fat and sinews. Rinse eggplant, discard stem, and cut rest into 1-inch cubes. Peel onions and chop. Peel ginger and grate. Rinse chile peppers, discard stems, and slice rest thinly. Rinse and core tomatoes, and cut into eighths.

Heat clarified butter in a dutch oven, and sauté spices for about 1 minute. Add eggplant and sauté briefly. Stir in onions, ginger, and chiles. Add lamb and lentils, and sauté briefly.

Stir in tomatoes, 2 cups water (or stock), lemon juice, and sugar. Cover and simmer over medium heat for 1 hour or until lamb is tender, stirring occasionally. Salt to taste. Also, season with garam masala to taste.